Behind the Scenes

Behind the Scenes

HOW TO SURVIVE IN THE MOVIE BUSINESS
AS A
FREELANCE FILM TECHNICIAN

JOSEPH J. ALLEN

Your Author Journey Begins Here

Copyright © 2020, Joseph J. Allen

All rights reserved. Printed in the U.S.A.

No part of this publication may be reproduced or transmitted in any form or by any means, electronic or mechanical, including photocopy, recording or any information storage and retrieval system now known or to be invented, without permission in writing from the publisher, except by a reviewer who wishes to quote brief passages in connection with a review written for inclusion in a magazine, newspaper or broadcast.

Quantity Purchases:
Companies, professional groups, clubs, and other organizations may qualify for special terms when ordering quantities of this title. For information, email info@ebooks2go.net, or call (847) 598-1150 ext. 4141.
www.ebooks2go.net

Published in the United States
by ebooks2go, Inc.
1827 Walden Office Square, Suite 260, Schaumburg, IL 60173

ISBN: 978-1-5457-5307-1

*This book is dedicated to my
Mother and Father*

Table of Contents

Introduction ix

Chapter 1   The Hustle Game 1

Chapter 2   Do It All, See It All, Learn It All 7

Chapter 3   Movie Hours 11

Chapter 4   You Are Your Own Business 13

Chapter 5   Safety And Its Importance In The Business 17

Chapter 6   Sleep And Its Importance 21

Chapter 7   Other Useful Information As A Freelancer 23

Chapter 8   What Makes The Industry Fun 27

Chapter 9   Unions And How They Work 41

Chapter 10   Rates 47

Chapter 11   Hotel, Mileage, Zones And Per Diem 51

Chapter 12   Movie Equipment 53

Chapter 13	Movie Equipment Rental Business And How Film Shoots Come Together	55
Chapter 14	Freelancing And Balance	57
Chapter 15	Departments On A Movie Set And How They Work	59
Chapter 16	Freelance Additional Crew And Equipment—Cranes, Lighting, Crew	81
Chapter 17	Tools For The Freelance Film Technician	83
Chapter 18	Go At It And Have Fun	93
Chapter 19	Other Useful Information And Nuggets Of Wisdom	95

Acknowledgments 97

About The Author 99

Introduction

How did I get into the film business? I've always said once you get in the business ask people on set how they got their start. No two people will tell the same story. Each person's story will be guaranteed to have some interesting twists and turns of how they got to where they are at that very moment. My own story is no exception. Upon graduating from UCLA, I was undecided about a career choice, so I decided to go travel the world off and on for about five years. I'd travel, come home, pick up a job, make more money and then plan my next trip. It was a formidable time in my life. I was seeking. Learning. Seeing. It was my time to explore and find what I really enjoyed. By twenty-eight years old I had traveled to twenty-two countries. But while on my last trip to Central America, I felt the need to fulfill something inside me. I realized that I wanted to learn a trade.

So I cut my trip short, flew home and decided I was either going to apply to law school or try to get into the movie business in San Francisco. I reached out to my brother, who worked at the time for Lucasfilm as a rerecording sound mixer. I told him what I wanted to do and he said we should sit down and talk. That conversation set me on my path. In my eyes, my brother was someone who had made it in the business and was in many ways a mentor. It was from that discussion and my own research on both professions, I decided to forego law school and focus on trying to get into the movie business.

At this point, I was not some young kid out of college. I had worked in the wine business as a sales rep, in software sales, and in a law firm as an investigator. I had real-world experience. But nothing work wise had grabbed me until this idea. My brother reached out to a few of his contacts and an opportunity arose. It was an opening in a studio producing a stop-motion animation children's show for ABC Television. The opportunity was a production assistant/runner. Since I had no experience, this position was a typical start for many in the movie business. I sat down with the studio's producer, and she explained the position and my weekly rate. I quickly realized my bank account was not going anywhere for a while. So, after much thought and many sighs, I decided to sign on for the position. At twenty-eight years old, I started at the bottom. I quickly took hold of the job and learned the ropes. I was given my own truck and an amount of cash to go around San Francisco and get things for each studio department. I liked to drive, so I looked at it as an opportunity to get paid to explore. I began to learn the city layout and enjoy my work. I quickly learned the cool places to go and the places that all the film people frequented. I started to meet people and learn. Within a year

I began to gain traction. I got promoted several times from production assistant to editing to stage assistant to camera assistant. The lesson here is many coming into the business will have to start the same way—at the bottom. Attitude and work ethic will define you no matter where you begin. Strength and patience in both of these areas will allow, with time, upward movement.

After a year at the studio I started at, ABC Television execs flew up from Los Angeles and cancelled production. So it was time to begin again. After putting out feelers for work, I got on to a small independent movie as a grip. When we finished filming the movie, I gave my resume to the director of photography with the hope he might bring me on to other films in the future. A month later, while out of work and still wondering if this business was the best decision for me, I got a call from the San Francisco motion picture union president asking if I'd be interested in working on a movie in town. That call was on to a union movie called *Phenomenon*, with John Travolta, Forest Whitaker, and Robert Duvall. Twenty-five plus years later, I'm still going. Still having fun. Still learning. Still meeting lots of great people. And still hustling. Every person's tenure in the business is different. Some people come in and out of the business within a year. I am now in my twenty-fifth year in the industry. The magic is still there for me, and keeps me coming back.

I have always gone out of my way to help new people and anyone else interested that I encounter to try and get a break into the business. I've always liked to demystify the movie business for people. Many people ask me all the time how the business works or to tell them what cool thing I've been working on. I've always tried to help people understand the complicated machine that exists behind the camera. It takes an army to make a movie. It is a well-oiled machine, where each technician knows their part and does it with great artistry. As a result, magic is created on screen. Within that magic exists unusual occurrences, stories, spectacular stunts, fights, things gone wrong, monster personalities, inequalities, things that people thought couldn't be done, egos, incredible machinery, magnificent things built, fun, laughter, and more visual candy than you could ever imagine. Even industry people are fascinated by things that go on behind the scenes. It's always been about the stories, the work and the visual magic and it always will be.

To me behind the scenes was where it was the most interesting and still remains this way. It's not based on your looks in front of the camera. It's based on your intelligence, creativity and what you can do with your hands. It's a trade, and a very cool one at that. You get to be a part of making films, whether that is a thirty-second commercial or a feature film that will be seen by millions and generations. It's a unique industry filled with many unique people. If you follow some of the advice I offer in this book, you can and will have your own interesting journey in the business. Good luck, and I wish you the best!

Chapter 1

The Hustle Game

It's time to hit the ground running and get aggressive. The freelance game is all about hustle. And hustle these days is getting your name, any way you can, in front of people that are in the business and working.

There are a few ways to approach networking:
- The old-school method includes finding a way to meet industry people either at a job or through a contact. Someone always knows someone in the business.
- Seek out young filmmakers and work on their films for free to gain experience.
- Set up a phone call to introduce yourself and ask them the most important question: "Do you have any projects I could help out with?"
- Another option is to go to the union hall of the union you are interested in—if you plan on trying to go union—and turn in your resume. Ask if they have any work available? It's not

unheard of that they may send you out on a job right then and there. More on unions and how they work later in the book.

- Get a copy of the film directory in your local town. San Francisco has one called the *Reel Directory*, and they advertise craftsmanship for hire. Get a copy and start calling all the people listed in your field of interest. Be sure to have good information gathering questions prepared. And don't be afraid to ask for an opportunity to work on any upcoming work.

- Contact all film rental houses and ask if they have any jobs going out that they need crew. Ask them if they can tell you the name and numbers of some local key people that work frequently. Once you get those numbers, call and follow the same tips as stated above. Or send an introductory text and ask if they have projects they need help with.

The key is hustle. If you're not hustling to get your name out there, then the phone won't ring. Freelance work and temporary work within the industry is not for everyone. It takes a certain type of person to deal with the ups and downs of the business. You have to be mentally tough when work gets slow and believe that you will be working when the work picks back up. My advice to anyone starting out is to use these methods I list above. But also have other part time or full time work to keep money coming in until you get established.

People come into the business at different ages. If you are in your twenties, your tolerance for not making a lot of money is much higher, mostly because you're coming out of college and used to being broke. Usually young kids in the business don't have a house, family and other things to support and can handle lower wages in the beginning. As you start to get some experience, your rates will start to increase, along with your knowledge of how rates work and fluctuate between movies and commercial filmmaking.

One thing to think about as you start to get more work is how you want to structure your freelance work. Some in the business do not like doing television commercials because they are not consistent. You may be working on a TV commercial three days one week, one day the next, seven days the following and then nothing for two weeks. These schedules fluctuate all the time. But if you are on a TV show or movie, those projects operate on a set schedule and time frame. For example, television shows will usually come into a city and film anywhere from a few days or a few months. If the TV show is filming the entire show in a city, a full television episode takes seven days to film.

For television shows, the studio will have a pilot to shoot first to see how it looks and if audiences like it. If green lit, then the studio will begin filming a certain amount of episodes to complete season one. That said, any crew that gets hired on the pilot usually has a steady job for as long as the show runs. Sometimes that can end up being a multi year run of work. Working on television shows usually will be six to nine months of shooting. They then take a hiatus, come back and run the same length of time for season two and so on. Again, the attraction is that it is steady weekly work for a freelance technician. Television hours often are very long—anywhere from ten to eighteen hours a day. A regular week can run anywhere from five to seven days and then start all over again. So, as you can see, it can get rather grueling.

Feature films are a bit different. They come into a city and usually film anywhere from two weeks to nine months or more. If it's a blockbuster feature film from Hollywood of two hundred million plus, usually it will be in the city for a long period of time and have massive crews working on it. The same theory applies to working on a large feature film as a television show. It's steady work for a freelancer. The added benefit for many technicians is the stockpiling union hours and money toward their benefits. This is a very important thing for anyone that is a permit technician or journeyman union member.

Some other options for the freelance film technician to think about are working corporate interviews, documentary projects, live action sports or television commercials. All these last scenarios are less consistent. My advice is to be open to anything that comes your way. You never know what a call or text may offer you for a job. That is what keeps it exciting. Try to narrow down what you enjoy doing in the business and focus on getting really good at that. But also, always be open to learning other positions in the beginning. It will only make you stronger as a technician.

One thing you must be open to as a freelancer is the ability to adapt and change. You may hit traction with a crew and be working in the niche of the business that you want at any point. It's often that this happens and you just roll from movie to movie with them. It can be a wonderful experience and a lot of fun that can last for years—travel, cool projects, and new and interesting work all the time. But I urge you to always be on your game. Know that the ride can change at any moment, and you have to have the ability to adapt and change when it does. For no reason at all the group you worked with for years might just stop calling you to do projects. I stress the importance of always networking on every job. Because if one avenue of work goes away for an unknown reason, you have the ability to put fifteen calls or texts out to other sources of work and be working the next day. This is the nature of the business.

As fun and exciting as it is, things change all the time. Some people rise faster than you to higher ranking positions. Never let that grind on you. It's the path they are on. Celebrate their successes, encourage them and learn from it. Keep yourself up and positive. Once your reputation is set in place as a fun, smart, and consistent technician, then you'll always have work available to you in some fashion. Be open to possibilities. They can be in front of you every day if you pay attention. It can happen this quickly, you meet someone new on set and they are moving on to a project and pull you on to it because they need help. Keep your eyes and ears open. You will be amazed at what you hear and learn. And if you are savvy, you will learn a lot just by listening.

Chapter 2

Do It All, See It All, Learn It All

As a freelance technician, in the beginning, you're unknown to everyone. Sure, you may know someone in the business. And you likely reached out to them, and they possibly helped you get your first break. Great! Most new technicians come into the business with little to no experience. It's important in the beginning to come in humble, hungry and with your eyes wide open.

Once on a movie set, look around you. Watch the machine at work. Big budget movies on average are funded for millions of dollars. With that comes big equipment, big crews to run it, big scenes and a big script that sometimes can take a month or years to finish filming. Your first time on set can feel both exciting and overwhelming.

Depending what position you've been hired for, you'll most likely feel lost. And that's OK. Everyone has to start somewhere. Your three best friends in the business are a good attitude, the ability to get your hands dirty and a gritty work ethic. These three characteristics will always get you noticed and get you hired back. For me, I've always tried to help new kids coming into the business. I try to go out of my way to introduce myself to them and give them industry advice. I have been in the business long enough to see young talent that will rise up through the ranks—the kid who is at the lowest position, making the least amount per day but hungry for the *work*, hungry to learn, hungry to tackle all tasks with a good attitude, and is a workhorse. That is the kid who will get noticed and start the ascent in the business.

People come into the business at various ages of life. I came into the business at age twenty-eight. There is no age requirement. If you use the above information, you will always be working no matter what age you start in the industry. In the beginning of your career, it's important to get comfortable saying yes to pretty much every job that comes your way. First of all, that is a great way to begin to learn many things. The business is filled with many talented and creative people. For each job you are hired to do, use my age-old rule of thumb: Shadow the best person on the job. Watch everything they do, how they do it, how they communicate, what tools they use, their work ethic, techniques, and then ask them intelligent questions. At the end of the day, take notes on what you've learned. Study them, then apply what you've learned. As time pushes forward, and you get a few years under your belt in the industry, you can start to really think about which department you like best. Talk to the key people running those departments and express your interest in joining them if an opportunity arises. As long as you carry with you the above-mentioned qualities, you'll be on your way.

Chapter 3

Movie Hours

Movie business hours are not nine to five! That has to be emphasized right out of the gates. I'm sure as a kid you heard rumors or read about doctors and lawyers having really long hours, and that's true. The movie business is no different. Movie and television hours are on average anywhere from eight hours to eighteen hours per day. Television and movies are widely known for very long days of filming. They are based on an eight-hour-a-day minimum, and any time over the eight hours is overtime to twelve hours and double time after twelve hours. Television commercials are based on a ten-hour day minimum, meaning that you are hired for your rate based off a ten-hour minimum. If you go over ten hours, the same rules mentioned above apply.

Some important things to remember: The hours are long, and the business is a blue-collar business. You have to be comfortable getting your hands dirty and constantly moving during all hours. A running motto in the business is hurry up and wait. It rings true in that when you're prepping to light a scene or under a timeline to get work done, you're hauling ass to finish. Once complete, the pace slows and you can chill out a bit until the next project comes forth.

Chapter 4

You Are Your Own Business

The title says it all. As a person considering getting into freelancing on films, this is an important chapter to pay attention to. A quote in the business among freelancers is: "You are only as good as your last job." This means that no matter how well you did on your last job, and no matter how great everyone praised your work, that job is over, and now you have to try and find more work. For many starting out in the freelance world, that is a scary proposition. Young or old, it can be very stressful when the phone doesn't ring and the bills start piling up. This is one big reason why you must always be a hustler in the business and why your relationship skills become essential. This is the time you need to hit the ground running and be making calls. Go to the union hall, text friends or be working on your own projects. Your down time is as important as your up time. Your down time is the time you need to focus on yourself as a business and how to get your name out there in front of people. Never forget the power of going after something you want to do.

As your own business you must pay attention to what it means to be your own business. What I mean by that is that as you start to gain traction in the business and start working more, there are things you are going to need to think about. For example, I would recommend you immediately talk to people around you about finding a good tax accountant. In any given year in the business you can work for anywhere between thirty to fifty employers. That can get very overwhelming if you're trying to do your taxes yourself. Talk to people in the business and find out who they use. Additionally, I suggest as quickly as possible, getting assets in your corner such as real estate, movie equipment or any other type of asset you may want to go after. Assets are pivotal to have and use as a write off against your high income.

As much as you may learn by being on the job, it is your responsibility as your own business to seek out answers for yourself to the many questions and mysteries of the business. As I mentioned before, the business is a mystery to many. Not only on the outside but also people on the inside. The only reason I feel people on the inside feel it's a mystery is because they don't ask questions and figure the game out on their own. And for those that don't, they usually have a short-lived duration of time as a freelancer. It is a tough business, and unless you have a tough mindset and thick skin, you'll not survive.

As your own business, you are the CEO. The head honcho. Mr. Big Shot. And as the guy in charge of yourself and your company, you must be good at many things. The things you need to be good at are: being resourceful, amiable, strong, smart, a quick study, frugal and always trying to learn more. There is another great saying in the business: "Be nice to them on your way up because you're going to see them on the way down." That is a very true saying. As much hustle as you put into freelancing, never forget that you always need to be a people person. Have the ability to get along with others. No one likes working with jerks. And for the most part, jerks usually end up offending so many people that no one wants to work with them and the calls for work stop going to them. Thus they either faze completely out of that market or they go to another market and see if they can work there. But more than likely, your reputation will follow you wherever you go. So pay close attention to how you act and deal with people. You may think that going from one market to the next will allow you to escape bad behavior. I assure you it will not. It is a small world and a small community of people behind the camera. People talk and with communication so accessible, it is very easy to send a text and ask, "What is this person like and are they good?" Everyone is connected. So just be sure you do a good job, have a great attitude and be fun to work around. The rest will take care of itself.

Chapter 5

Safety And Its Importance In The Business

Safety in the business is huge and sometimes can be neglected in a hurry. Almost like clockwork, on big movies, first thing in the morning the assistant director will call for a safety meeting. At this meeting the entire crew is gathered to listen to the safety concerns about the day of shooting ahead. The AD will carefully lay out and explain the day if it is a day with stunts, explosions and/or any other highly dangerous scene that will be filmed. It is a chance for the entire crew to listen to what will be happening and ask questions. It's important to note that on big movie sets there are a lot of moving parts and lots of people doing the jobs that need to be done in order to make the film happen. On the bigger film sets there is always a medic on set. The medic will be introduced at this meeting so that everyone knows who this person is at the header of the day.

Large crews combined with long hours and five to seven day weeks begin to add up over time. People get tired.

Fast. Especially if they are not getting enough sleep depending on their own circumstances at home and how they get to work. Many people commute to and from location every day. For some, it is a two hour commute one way to set, then work a sixteen hour day, then drive home, then do it all over again the next day. That's twenty hours and therefore, leaving four hours of turnaround and sleep. I think you get the picture. Exhaustion starts to set in and where someone may be ultra alert one day, on another day that may not be the case. As a crew member, it is your responsibility always to be aware of your surroundings and crew for unsafe situations. If there is ever an unsafe situation that you see or hear about, go talk to the AD or your key person and bring it to someone's attention immediately. It could save someone's life or your own.

Over the years, there have been instances in the business of people getting killed through negligence, exhaustion or no one checking if a situation is safe or legal to do. I cannot urge you enough about being aware. As fun as the business is, it is a dangerous business as well with the many things that are done to make a film. For example, special effects explosions, car stunts, gun battles, cranes, heavy equipment, moveable large sets, etc., are just some of the things that are dangerous that all crew need to be aware of. Other things to note, smaller shoots often do not have a medic with them. They are called splinter units of a movie or it's just a smaller movie with smaller crews and budget. With the smaller movie, it is usually crewed up with newer people in the business who don't have as much experience but are trying to learn and get a break on to bigger projects. There are times that things are moving so fast on these particular projects that safety can take a back seat. If you ever have someone pushing you to do something unsafe, stop and think about what it is they are asking you to do. Chances are if your gut is telling you it doesn't feel right, then don't do it. Your life is more important than one potentially stupid thing you are being asked to do. Tell the person you are not comfortable doing it and go talk to the AD or your key. Or if it's both of them asking you to do it, don't and either tell them you're not comfortable doing it or leave the project. Never feel as if you can't leave a project due to personal reasons whatever those may be. If the project is a complete disaster and disorganized, then maybe it's just not the project for you to be a part of. That is where the power of saying you're not available is yours for additional work days if asked back. Some projects are like that due to the nature of the script content, egos or conflicts with the way the project or crews are being run. Your enjoyment of the business will wholeheartedly run exclusively on your ability to keep yourself safe and others safe by being alert at all times.

It's also worth noting for new freelancers entering the business to never ever run a movie set. Nothing is so important that you need to run for anyone! You are not saving lives. Walk fast and with intent. No one will ever fault you for that. I have watched so many young kids come into the business and all day long they are running one direction and then the other. After a few hours of watching that, I will stop them and have a quick discussion on walking versus running. Most of them get it and the running stops. But some continue to do it and it makes them look ridiculous and also is dangerous. As I mentioned, there are a lot of moving parts on a movie set. Those who choose to run on a set are inevitably going to either trip, run into someone carrying something, or cause some other disaster. Don't run. The last note on this subject is another age-old adage in the business: "Running makes you look like you don't know what you're doing."

Chapter 6

Sleep And Its Importance

The importance of getting enough sleep cannot be said enough. Working these kinds of hours for days and weeks on end can be extremely grueling. And if you don't pay attention to your body, it can be extremely dangerous. What do I mean? There are numerous unfortunate examples of technicians driving back from sets after working sixteen-hour plus days and falling asleep at the wheel and getting seriously hurt or killed. This is *not* what you want to happen and I highly advise paying close attention to getting eight hours of sleep or more when into long grueling schedules. Skip going out to party with your buddies on a particular night if you are wasted tired. It will take you days to recover if you are working weeks upon weeks of sixteen-hour days. Another reminder and safety note to think about is that the hours I speak about above are your on-set work hours. That is not even including whatever hours it takes you to get from your house to set and then back again. So whatever that time is, add to the hours of your day and you'll see exactly what I'm talking about with regards to getting enough sleep. I cannot stress this enough. Be smart. Be careful. Think. And pay attention to what your body is telling you. A few tricks to help you get to work and home safely are: strong coffee, loud music, roll the windows down, chew gum, five hour energy and then more coffee! Or just pull over and take a nap if the above is not working!

Chapter 7

Other Useful Information As A Freelancer

Anyone that is coming in new to the business should think about a few of the things I'm going to mention here. Freelance work can be flush, and the next week it can go quiet for a period of time. So for anyone starting out in the business, it's important to remember to have other sources of income in the slow times, whether that is part-time work you do while trying to get into more steady film work or other sources of income. One should always be thinking about ways to keep money coming in.

When you are young starting out in the business, it is important to go after and say yes to almost all jobs coming through the door for you. Be able to put other less important things on hold until you start to get some traction as a freelancer and more calls start coming in. Be prepared for that timeline to be roughly one to two years.

For some, they hit the ground running and never look back. The combination of the right timing, their talent, hard work and persistence make it so they are immediately in, working and known. For others, that is not the case. Even with the most talented person and great attitude, they can struggle to get traction in a particular market. Do not give up! It will happen; it just takes persistence and hitting all the angles you can think of to try and get a break.

Remember, as a freelancer, you get hired for a particular job. The job could last three days or three months. But when it ends, you don't know when the phone will ring again. It could be the next day or the next month. So always be prepared to be hustling to move from project to project. One thing that I have done through the years is focus on diversification. I have purchased real estate, invested in the stock market, own movie rental equipment and worked tirelessly on creative side hustles that I hope to bring to the market. Again, the focus here is to try and make you are aware that you should always be thinking of ways to survive and thrive. This becomes even more important once you have a family. The hustle game gets turned up a notch. You now have to provide for your family and whomever else you take care of. So pay attention to these details and be smart in your approach to your work.

"It pays to be prepared." I grew up involved in Boy Scouts of America. I'm an Eagle Scout and this saying was drilled into our heads before going into the Sierras on major hikes. I happened to be lucky enough to be part of one of the best troops in the entire Bay Area.

We were known for how tough we were at competitions against other troops. We would train for months beforehand and go in and crush the competition at all the field events. This is where I got really good at survival techniques, knot tying, mental toughness and my love of the outdoors. Much of this training transferred over into the movie business for me. It is a lot of the same type of work, people and mental mindset. So I instantly fell in love with the business from this standpoint. Being prepared in the business is not unlike anything else you do in life. It's important to remember that every job you go out on will throw different variables at you, such as weather conditions, gear needed and terrain of where you are filming. The prepared person in these above categories is always ahead of the game over others. While others are scrambling to cover their asses because they didn't think ahead, you can always be calm knowing you did.

Another important aspect that one needs to remember is staying up with technology. You don't have to learn every little detail of the newest technology that is being released. But it will serve you well to keep your pulse on new gear hitting the market and becoming popular. New lighting, cameras, grip gear, rigging gear, and the like. The more you know, the stronger you are as a technician. So once again, pay attention. Ask questions. Learn. Practice. As a side note, it's not just new gear hitting the market that you should be aware of. As a technician, there will be gear and the way things are done as a department that you will have to learn. Gear for films is made by some of the best engineers and mechanics in the world. And it's made to last. As an example, there is a lot of gear used in the grip department that is well over twenty years old and still does what it was intended. Learn the gear. Be aggressive in doing your research. Do it on set. Do it off set. Throw yourself into learning. Every job you go out on you will see someone do something that maybe you've seen done a hundred times one way and they do it one time better and faster. So if you see them do something like that, ask them how they did it. Have them teach you. Learn and then go do it yourself when it applies.

Another tip: Do not let anyone roll over you. Ever. You'll meet hundreds of people in a given year. And many new people per job. You'll constantly be tested by different personalities on a given set. Some within your department, some not. You must keep the ability to get along with others in your back pocket at all times. If a problem arises, work through it calmly to a resolution. Getting into an argument proves nothing and no one wins. Look to find solutions. And if things escalate, choose to either walk away and let someone else deal with this person or sometimes (not often) it is time to put someone in their place. I've mentioned it before, do not let people walk on you or roll over you. And most importantly, do not let someone disrespect you verbally. If that is the case, take care of that then and there. I tell my sons this all the time. There is a time to flick on your "asshole switch" and take care of an egotistical person, no matter what their title is. Once accomplished, turn off your "asshole switch" and go back to being a nice person. That is what people will remember. Nice guys win. Be real. Be humble. Be strong.

Chapter 8

What Makes The Industry Fun?

What makes the industry fun you ask? A ton of stuff! Let me explain, first and foremost, you get to wear what you want. It doesn't matter if it's thirty degrees outside. If you want to wear shorts, a Hawaiian shirt, a cowboy hat, and Doc Martens, no problem. Behind the scenes is not based on how you look but how you get along with people, your work ethic and how quickly you can get the work done while having fun.

The movie industry will take you to fantastic local destinations and far away destinations. What makes movies powerfully grand and beautiful are landscapes as backdrops to a script. Depending on the script, location scouts will search out vistas, homes, mountain locations, roads and cities to film in. One of the great things about working on films is that you get to go to and work at these amazing places that many never get to see.

Getting into the movie business you can do at any age, as I mentioned before. I got into the business at age twenty-eight. I have many friends who are in their fifties, sixties, and even seventies still in the business. Why, you ask? Because they love what they do, not because they have to be there. Many come in from all walks of life having done many professions prior. The people with prior life experience can play well in many scenarios. From the ability to work equipment to dealing with people, you don't need a film degree to begin in the business. You just need to have an interest and then follow the many steps of advice I give within this book.

One of the greatest perks to the movie business- free food. Whether it be a television show, movie, or commercial, all crew is treated by production to a fully catered breakfast, lunch and dinner during filming. You show up to work and find the caterer who has stations set up for anything you can imagine for breakfast. It's like being a kid in a candy shop honestly. And if you get carried away, you can gain ten pounds in a week. No joke. But thankfully the work is physical, and you work that right off. And as if catered meals aren't enough, you also get what's called craft service. That is a department that specializes in feeding the crew when the catered meals are done.

Some other great perks are what's called swag. Swag is given by productions to the crew as thank-you's for all the hard work they did on a given movie. Some examples I've been given through the years have been: movie jackets, T-shirts, hats, pins, stickers, briefcases, bags and tools. Oftentimes each of the above items are printed with the film's name and your name on it as well. Depending on the movie, some of these items can go on to be very valuable. Just remember that if you get some unique piece of memorabilia, hold on to it. The movie business is one of the most lucrative businesses in the world and there is a mystique to many about it and how it's done. Additionally, movies touch people worldwide. There are many collectors out there for particular movies they love. So they will often pay a lot of money for a certain piece of memorabilia from their favorite film.

Working on films is fun. But what's the work really like? It can be outside, inside, on the ocean, under the ocean, in the mountains, on mountains, in the snow, rain, blazing heat, crazy winds, high surf, on stages, in tanks, on boats, trains, trucks, motorcycles, freeways, helicopters, rivers, and the list goes on. The work is not for the faint of heart. You have to be tough, gritty, a quick study of conditions, a survivor, have thick skin, carry a lot of tools, be strong, be able to get along with people, and most of all enjoy the process. It beats staring at a computer all day. You are judged by what you can do with your mind and creativity versus how you look and what you are wearing. To me, the greatest perk working behind the scenes has always been to wear what you want and work outside.

Photo captured by surf photographer Frank Quirarte while filming feature film "Chasing Mavericks" in Half Moon Bay, California. A rogue wave hit our boat nearly flipping it. The 65 foot boat was being used as the camera mounting boat for 2nd Unit on the film. I'm in the red jacket on the port side and stern of the boat.

Shooting a crane shot on "Rise of the Planet of The Apes" in San Francisco, California. Photo credit-Henry Nguyen.

On the set of "The Matrix Reloaded" in Alameda, California. San Francisco/Los Angeles Grip and Camera Crews enjoying one of the many fun moments of this picture.

On the set of HBO feature film Hemingway & Gellhorn with a prop Marlin. San Francisco, California.

Panoramic crane moves on a secret film project in Yosemite, California. Photo credit-Riley Miller.

Bringing motion to camera, pictured here on a Chapman Super Nova crane bucket raising 8 cameras rigged to truss for an Under Armour commercial with NBA basketball star Steph Curry. Oakland, California.

Enjoying a moment of rest after rigging a large overhead truss for a commercial in Vallejo, California.

Long term friendships in the business are what it's all about. Coming up through the ranks with these guys has been awesome. They are like family and I never tire of getting to work with them for the laughs and fun projects. Pictured from left to right: Jay Coakley, Todd Stoneman, Gordon McIver, Joe Allen, Jason Predock-Vallejo, California.

Rigging cameras for a stunt scene on the feature film "Ant-Man and the Wasp" in San Francisco, California.

Working with feature film star "Chopper-the dog" on a commercial. This dog had me laughing all day long with his antics. I had to get a photo with him and he did not disappoint. San Francisco, California.

Chapter 9

Unions And How They Work

Unions are a major component for work and to protect movie technicians when working on a live action film. They provide a set hourly wage, vacation pay included with your hourly wage, and health and pension benefits. Benefits are paid in and on your behalf for each hour worked. They also provide contracts with built-in protections against the studios or production companies if they do not provide agreed upon terms within the contract. An example of that could be not breaking you for a meal after six hours. Therefore, each half hour increment of time that they continue to not break you for a sit down meal they're penalized. This penalty is known as a meal penalty (MP) on paper and equates to a monetary amount that you get paid until they break you for a meal. Sometimes that can equate to hundreds of dollars on top of your daily wage. There are rules and regulations that the studios and unions have worked out and are set in stone within film contracts.

Any break from the set contract wording by the production and that equates to an action on behalf of the union to protect the technician. So you begin to see the importance of being union on a movie for the protections and benefits when you are working. The health benefits are a monetary amount, once you qualify. You should check with your union for specifics to qualify. This is a massive benefit of being part of the union. Once you get the health benefits, one should work hard to keep them or it's considered a break in service, and you have to start all over again. It's always in your best interest to be versed as deeply as you can in the inner workings of the union, contracts and rules when on a film—any film!

Getting into motion picture unions though is not as easy as you might think. You don't just show up at their door and they put you to work. Although, that said, I do know friends of mine that that has happened to. So it is not out of the question. For the most part, it is a challenging and sometimes very long, arduous process to get in and get steady work from movie unions. It's a timing thing, like many things in life.

Certain markets for unions are tougher than others and the process to get in varies greatly from one to the next. For example, trying to get into the Los Angeles film trade unions are different from the way to get into the San Francisco film trade union. Some of the nuances of getting into the Los Angeles unions are that you need to work thirty days on a union show in order to become a union member. So you have to get lucky to be asked to be on a union movie and be able to make it to the thirty-day mark to get into the union. I know many people who got hired on to a union movie only to be cut loose on day twenty-nine, thus not getting in and having to try all over again for another union movie. If you are trying to work television commercials, the competition is even more fierce and competitive for the jobs but not impossible. Again, persistence is your friend.

Unions across the country differ. What I mean by that is that, most unions that are specific to the movie industry are exactly that, specific to the movie industry. For example, Los Angeles movie unions such as Local 80-Motion Picture Studio Grips or Local 728-Motion Picture Studio Electricians work exclusively as a grip or electrician when given a job from the union hall. But there are exceptions to this rule with a select group of mixed unions that do not operate this way.

One such example is Local 16 out of San Francisco. It is a mixed union of work, meaning that not only does it rule the San Francisco jurisdiction of film contracts and technicians hired on to films but also provides work in many other areas for union members. Some examples would be rock and roll concerts, corporate events and any other large entertainment event that comes through or within the San Francisco union jurisdiction. Also, another benefit of Local 16 as a mixed local versus say Local 80, which only does movie grip work, means that you can work many different positions on a film or position of work they offer. For example, one day you could be a movie grip on a film, and the next day be sent out as a movie electrician. The following day you could be sent out as a special effects technician. The day after that you could be sent out as a pre-rig grip. Get the point? I have always thought it to be a great aspect to Local 16 that you get to learn and be a part of many different trades on a movie set or within other entertainment events. That to me was something appealing because there are so many talented technicians in the union to learn from. The more knowledge you learn, the stronger technician you become overall as your experience grows.

Historically, Local 16 is a very difficult union to get into. I am going to give you the rundown of the steps to get hired out of this union in San Francisco. It does not work as Los Angeles, nor any other city for that matter, as to how you get in. First, you have to submit a resume online to the Local 16 website, and then you go in and see if they have work available. You should also follow up your resume with phone calls. Alternatively, you could have a current Local 16 member vouch for you as a technician, and hope they permit you to work. By permitting you to work, I mean that if the union is busy, they would contact you and tell you they want to put you on a job. You would take a job and then later fill out paperwork at the hall. By allowing you to work in their jurisdiction, you become what's known as a "permit technician." Although not a journeyman, the permit worker is allowed to work in and for the union and will accrue benefits. It's important to note that when work gets slow, permit workers are the last to get called out onto jobs. Journeymen always take precedence. As a side note, it is not completely necessary that you have movie experience on your resume but something film or technician related is helpful. Your resume stays in the system for six months. Often, it comes down to how you present yourself in person, how dynamic you are, and how persistent you are in getting yourself in front of key hiring people that will get you noticed and working.

Another added benefit of working for a union is the pension. Each hour of service equates to a percentage of money going toward a pension in your name. If you continue to work long enough for the union, you will start to accrue a monetary amount that will be paid in monthly installments when you reach retirement age. This may not seem like a big deal. But trust me it is. This source of income will be paid to you when you retire and that is something you can rely on for all the years of hard work you put in. Don't ignore it.

Keep in mind, by not going union, you would not be able to work TV shows or movies in whatever city because all large scale productions are ninety percent union. Additionally, working outside the lines of being union would mean that you are paying for your own health benefits and without contractual protections on certain projects. My suggestion is to always talk to people and ask questions to get the answers of how to work in the niche of the business you want to be in. Get the answers and weigh the pros and cons.

Chapter 10

Rates

Rates for movies and television are relatively the same except in certain circumstances with television. Again, as discussed, almost all movies and television shows are union. The unions negotiate with the studios in advance of shooting what the rates are going to be. For movies they're a negotiated hourly rate for all technicians with a sliding scale from top position to the last position on a specific crew. As previously mentioned, all union movies fall under a motion picture contract that protects the technician if there is a dispute over hours, overtime or any other contractual issue.

Other circumstances that would apply to a lower starting hourly rate would be for what's called a tier one, two, or three movie. These are usually smaller scale independent films that got backing and are being made in hopes of getting picked up by a larger studio for distribution. The rates of tier one, two, and three can be shockingly low, nearly half of what you'd be making hourly on a full rate feature film. The running joke is if you work on a tiered movie that when you get your paycheck they include a Kleenex for you to wipe away the tears from such low pay. Films like this are usually crewed up by the young technicians trying to make a name for themselves. While the more seasoned vets take on the bigger, more challenging and higher paying films.

The certain circumstances I refer to above are about union television pilots or shows. A television pilot is a concept show that the studio has green lit to shoot an episode that will then be aired to a private audience and studio heads. If they get a favorable response to the script and pilot, it will be green lit for a season one. And filming will begin. The catch is that with season one it is still somewhat of an experiment and the rates will not be at movie scale. Whatever studio is backing the show will negotiate a much lower scale hourly rate and if the show does well, meaning a season two, then rates will come back slightly higher. It usually takes up to season four to get up to what you make on a movie at hourly scale.

Commercials pay rates are the highest in the business. They are not paid hourly. Instead, they are paid via a day rate that is negotiated ahead of the shoot date. Most cities run with a standard ten-hour day rate per certain departments that increases every six months to a year. It usually sits significantly higher per hour than movie or television rates.

Everything you do in your career and as a freelancer requires your ability to sell yourself. You have to know how to politic and negotiate to get things you want.

So the better you are at communicating ideas to people, negotiating and then asking for what you want, the better you will be as a business and in the business. If you hit a wall and consistently get a no, then figure out another approach and try again. If you don't ask for what you want, then you will not get it. People are not mind readers. Approach the powers that be for the things you want or need done. Never be afraid of someone's title. Treat them with respect and kindness with your want and you will very likely get what you want. But I stress to you the value of negotiation being of utmost importance as a freelancer. You'll often have to negotiate rates or many other things on the spot. If you have no idea how to tactfully go about it, then more than likely you will not get a desired result. So learn how to be strong not only physically but also as a businessperson.

Chapter 11

Hotel, Mileage, Zones, And Per Diem

If you are lucky enough to be asked to do a project out of town or out of state, there are certain things that will need to be thought about and asked. How long is the project? What's the rate? Union or non union? Are hotels being covered with per diem? Are we in van shuttles? This is an important section to pay attention to. These days out of town, state or country projects are less and less but they do happen. And if you get a chance to be a part of one, do it. They are usually a ton of fun. Some of the above things should be explained more in detail first though before agreeing to anything. First and foremost, after saying yes to the project, get your rate. If it's a union TV or movie, you will be at union scale (i.e., the hourly contracted rate for the position you are hired for). If it's a commercial, you will need to negotiate your rate if you're the first hire or get in line with the rate of the gaffer for the project on his rate—grip and electric mirror each other in key rates. Hotels, per diem and mileage outside the zone are usually covered by production if you are self driving. The zone in San Francisco is a thirty-mile radius 360 degrees from the union hall main address. That means that you are responsible for getting to a location that films anywhere within that thirty-mile radius and production will not pay for mileage. Anything outside of that range, production will pay for at the going tax rate for mileage.

Chapter 12

Movie Equipment

This is where the magic lies with me. Movie equipment is unique with unique purposes. It's beautifully designed and built to last. Whether it's a camera, light, grip equipment or other movie equipment, each piece of equipment has been engineered for a specific purpose to help create a film. It takes hundreds of talented craftspeople and technicians to take the equipment and make movie magic with it. From day one in the business, I wanted to pursue being a camera operator. As mentioned in the intro, I started at a non union studio at the bottom and worked my way up from runner, assistant editor, stage production assistant to camera assistant working with WWII Mitchell cameras. That's where I fell in love with the equipment and that camera. I began to learn how to load them and work with 35 millimeter film. The more I was around film gear, the more deeply I dove into the companies that made the equipment, the movies made with the equipment and how they did it, lighting equipment, grip equipment, etc. The list goes on and on. I loved it all. And still do.

I took particular interest in rigging equipment on films. My first movie I went out as a grip and found I really enjoyed the grip department and what they did. The guys were cool and very similar to me in personality. I also liked the grip department because it was still working directly with the camera. The equipment was fascinating to learn, use and see how it all came together to create motion on film. And so my journey began in a new direction as I started to get hired more and more to go out on to grip crews. I loved it. It was fun, exciting and always new. And still to this day, it is exactly that. I get to do something very unique for a living. And I am forever grateful for the experiences and journey I've had and continue to have.

Chapter 13

Movie Equipment Rental Business And How Film Shoots Come Together

As you become more entrenched in the business, one thing you might want to think about is owning rental equipment. There are many opportunities for owning gear and getting it on to jobs as a rental business. Let me explain how this works. This process applies as a road map to almost all film productions. When productions come in from anywhere in the world, they do not bring the gear with them. Producers will reach out to a production coordinator to find local crews. The coordinator will then make contact with a first assistant director, director of photography, gaffer, key grip, prop master, and any other department head needed for the shoot. Contact will be made to start the ball rolling on getting crew together and figuring out logistics of a shoot. The next step is that the coordinator will start working with the director, producers, first assistant director, and location department on the script and preparing for what's called a location scout.

Generally, two scouts will take place. A director's scout is where the director will go out to the anticipated locations and see if they fill the need for how they want the project to look. Then the location scout with the key people listed above will take place, where everyone can look at the locations. It is this scout where the director and director of photography can visualize how they want to shoot it. The director of photography will then communicate with the gaffer about the lighting per location and the key grip about any camera movement, camera rigging or light manipulation needed per location. Each department head on the scout will get notes per location as to what is needed from their department and crew to make the shoot happen.

As mentioned, usually speaking, no production coming into a city to shoot will carry with them equipment. It is too costly and cumbersome to travel with it. So they'll rent all film gear from local film gear rental houses. The keys typically also will have some gear that they own and if the shoot calls for particular needed items, they can rent the gear on to the job. Once the gear needed for the shoot is decided, the gear will be called in or emailed in to the local film rental houses. At that point all gear will start to be put together and a total gear cost list to rent will be sent back to production. Production will work with the rental house at that point on the budget and logistics of getting the trucks and gear to set for the filming of the project.

Chapter 14

Freelancing And Balance

Burnout is an important thing to try to avoid for yourself in the business. Burnout can happen to anyone in life, but especially with the long hours of the movie business. The long days can make it so that you have a limited personal life, if you let it. The quest is to manage important things in your life. Whether that is the love of your life, mountain biking twice a week or watching your kids grow up. I have watched many people say yes to every movie and television show that came to town. They hold it up like a badge of honor. And yes, that's great that they get offered these jobs. However, when the day is done or during it, oftentimes I will see them on the job and can see the exhaustion and strain of taking on so much work. The exhaustion leads to burn out, lack of sleep, not seeing their kids in weeks, breaking up with their girlfriend—or worse, their wife—or not getting to do other passions they love to do in months. When I see or hear this, I'll try to pull them aside and have a heart-to-heart with them, even if I don't know them and even if it's just for five minutes or less. What I have to tell them could set in motion them really rethinking what is important in their lives and realigning things to make those important again. I always try to help young people in the business and seasoned vets see that it is so important to have balance in the business. I understand everyone has different overhead and responsibilities. But the most important thing to remember is that there is one thing you never get back, and that is time. So be careful about the projects you take and take the time to take care of the important things outside of work (i.e., your health, family, and sleep).

Chapter 15

Departments On A Movie Set And How They Work

Movies, television shows or commercials all have a certain formula of departments that make up the backbone of getting a film made. Each of these departments play a special role in making a film. And I will explain each and their importance on a set.

Camera

The camera department is in charge of all cameras for a movie. They also carry all needed accessories for the cameras including lenses, monitors for pulling focus, camera sticks, high hats, etc. The camera team works directly for the director of photography. The director of photography works exclusively with the director. Both will work together on how the film is to look based on the script, lighting, location and acting. For example, handheld camera shots are used for a "lots of energy feel." Long dolly or crane shots are used for dramatic movement.

If there are two, three or four cameras (i.e.,-typically called A cam, B cam, C cam & D cam) working on a set for a particular day, that requires a cameraman to operate each camera. And there is an assistant camera person to pull focus for each camera. Each camera will have its own lens package and grip assigned to them if the camera is to be on a dolly or have dolly moves during the day via the script. Camera crews consist of the director of photography, camera operator, first and second camera assistants, film loader, DIT (digital imaging technician) and digital utility.

Grip & Pre Rig Grip

One term that describes the grip department is a jack-of-all-trades on a movie set. They are these things rolled into one: carpenter, rigger, mechanic, engineer and creative problem solver. The grip department is a complicated department to describe in one sentence. The head position in charge of the grip department is called the key grip. His right hand man is called the best boy grip. The best boy grip is in charge of all man power, equipment and paperwork. The two main things the grip department are in charge of are: first, working directly with the director of photography to accomplish what kind of camera movement for the shots and or where the camera will be rigged to in order to capture whatever shot is needed.

The grip department carries a fully loaded forty foot truck trailer packed with grip gear to help achieve any type of camera movement wanted and or any type of camera rigged shot needed. If a long dolly shot was needed for a particular shot, the grips would lay down and level the dolly track. Following that they would muscle the camera dolly up the track. Camera would then be placed on the dolly and the dolly grip would start to work out the shot with the DP on the track consisting of specific speed, camera heights and distance to capture the action. The second main part of what the grips are responsible for is rigging the camera. The grips carry all equipment to rig cameras to very difficult places. For example, rigging them to high speed boats, trains, helicopters, cars, trucks, motorcycles and planes, to name just a few. Once the camera is rigged to these motion machines, the DP can then begin the work with his camera, grip, stunts and production team to pull off how the action shot needed will happen. Usually these shots are part of an action film and require quite a bit of time to rig properly and rehearse before pulling off. Safety is the number one goal of all departments involved but especially the grip department when rigging any camera for a scene.

Another very important aspect of the grip department is manipulating natural and artificial light on a set. For natural light, the key grip is responsible for working with the DP to watch the arc of the sun and how that affects a particular shot at a particular time of day they are shooting. Full sun on a set is not usually what is desired for an exterior shot. It is the grip department's job to "take down" the direct sun off a set and actor. By that I mean, we carry various types of materials and cloths that allow light to push through it and make the light of a scene look softer. We accomplish that by using different size frames such as 20' × 20', 12' × 12',

8' × 8', 6' × 6' or 4' × 4' and then tie in a particular diffusing material desired and size into one of the above size frames for the shot and then place the frame to diffuse the natural sun. Frames and diffusion materials like this are used by the grips and DP in both natural light and artificial light situations. The key to filming a particular scene is always about the lighting, shadows and the look. Grips use many other various tricks to reflect light back onto a set or an actor for a scene. Some of the tricks are mirrors, reflector boards, bounce cards and white bounce material that when the sun or artificial light hits it will bounce light back to a scene.

Along with diffusing light, the grip department also shapes natural or artificial light for a scene with many types of things. Such items for taking down light used by the grips are called flags, nets or other types of diffusion. All these mentioned items come in sizes that were mentioned in the paragraph prior and even smaller. To make that clearer, the electric department will run all power and lights to a scene via the DP and gaffer's discretion. The key grip will then work with the DP to discuss how the DP would like the lighting shaped. Lighting can be shaped many different ways for a scene and played with by the DP, gaffer, and key grip artistically to give a particular look to a scene. To give an example, for a lovemaking scene, most scenes of this nature are intense, lighting is minimal but shaped with flags, nets, and diffusion to create a soft, intense, and moody scene on camera.

The pre-rig grip department is a separate unit on movies that work ahead of the main shooting unit of the movie to get the grip work accomplished. Some scenes are so technical and involved that it may take the pre-rig grips and pre-rig electric units a full month or more to rig the needed items for the scene. Usually these units are on movie sets for both exterior shots and stage work. It is a fun unit. It is where as a grip technician you really get to see the massive scale of work that is involved in making a movie happen. It is also a great place to begin as a technician. You can learn a ton of useful information on how to rig correctly and safely within pre-rig departments. I highly recommend taking any job offered within these departments to learn.

Electric and Pre-Rig Electric

The electric department on a movie set is in charge of many different aspects of the movie. First and most important, electric provides power on the set. Second and equally important, they also provide lighting to a set and to each scene. The gaffer is the person in charge of the electric department. The best boy electric reports directly to the gaffer. All technicians under the gaffer are known as electricians and work the power, lights, and the set. The gaffer reports directly to the director of photography for their vision of the film. Light and lighting is a major component to making any movie, whether a movie is using all natural light (the sun) to light it or if it's all done by artificial lights (lights run off power). Lighting gives mood and life to film. When it comes to electricity, power and lights, the intricacies are very technical and important to how a movie gets made. On some movie sets, it takes massive amounts of power to run the huge lights that are lighting a scene. That is a technical orchestration that is figured out by the gaffer, the pre-rig gaffer and the electric crew. Lights have to be placed in many different places to get a look for a film. Some places include rooftops, condor lifts, beefy stands, cars, trucks, moving car rigs, etc. This is when the electric department will work hand in hand with the grip department to get the lights rigged and placed where they need to be to capture a shot.

Pre-rig electric department is in charge of going in before the shooting crew arrives with all power and lighting. Pre-rig crew is only used when there is so much work needed in advance of the scene that there would be no way for the shooting unit to get all the work done within a reasonable amount of time for the work of the day. So a pre-rig crew is sent in the day before usually or hours before to rig the power and lighting for the scene so that when the shooting crew arrives, they unload the truck, walk in, set up the camera and begin shooting.

Stunts

The stunt department is brought in on films where the script requires a fight scene, someone jumping out of a building, out of a plane, off a cliff or things of the like. Most stunt men and women are high performance athletes and train rigorously to pull off the kinds of stunts listed above. For the big stunts, such as jumping off a fifteen-story building, a stunt person could make what some make in a year—a lucrative payoff with a massive risk. For some, fear is not a factor. Adrenaline is the drug of choice for a lot of people that are associated with stunt teams. And to watch them do these incredible feats is nothing short of amazing.

Stunt Rigging

This department is a specialized unit that is brought in on large feature films to rig highly technical flying rigs to suspend stunt people doing a stunt for the film. What makes this department so critical is that one wrong calculation and someone could die. A film series that most will know where many stunt riggers were used is on The Matrix.

Many of the scenes in that film series required massive planning, rigs, rehearsals and people to pull it off. Most dangerous scenes that need to be done are where stunt people are brought in to do the scene instead of the actors. When you watch a film and see people fly through the air, off buildings, bridges, moving trucks, high-speed motorcycles, and cars then you know why stunt people are used.

Special Effects

The special effects department is in charge of all things where highly technical machinery is used to produce explosions, fire, water, wind, rain, heat, cold and rigging as an element needed for a particular scene. Special Effects units are tough as nails and come from wide and varied backgrounds as technicians. I have watched these guys do things on set that have left me telling stories for years. They are very talented and specialized units that are essential to heavy action feature films.

Props

The prop department is an important part of the look of any film. They are in charge of giving a look to each scene of a film. An example of what they do: take a blank room for a scene and turn it into a period room filled with period furniture and decor. It is amazing to watch a blank slate of a particular set go from nothing to spectacular, based on whatever the script calls for. Anything can be considered a prop for a movie set. For example, a prop could be a pen all the way up in size to a car or large animal.

Greens

The greens department is in charge of all plants, trees, and any other living plant life on a given set. The greenery is often beefed up at a location or on a stage set to give it the appearance of being more exotic or beautiful. Everything comes down to the set designer's wishes on how they want the look interpreted. Most often set construction, greens, set painters and props are all working hand in hand getting a set ready for days, weeks or months in advance before the first unit lands to start filming.

Construction

Set construction is an integral part of movie making. They are in charge of building a set or sets for scenes to be filmed. Some sets are built to replicate locations or match an architectural look desired for the script. Construction, in some instances, can and will build a whole town where there was none before. An example of this would be in the desert, in order to shoot a western.

Construction will build sets for exterior locations or on a stage for long term shooting. Sets built on a stage allow production to film for unlimited amounts of time and get all the shot coverage and footage they need for the film. Personally this department never fails to amaze me with what they build for any given movie. This department can be a fantastic place to begin as a technician.

Set Painters

Set painters are another very important aspect to moviemaking. Once a set has been built, the set painters will come in and paint a set to the appropriate color and tones called for in the script. The set painters are extremely talented at what they do. They can make a room or object that is new look like it's one hundred years old through paint and technique. This effectively sets the tone and mood, along with lighting which becomes spectacular on film. I never tire of walking onto a movie set and seeing the amazing things that have been created.

Script Supervisor

The script supervisor is in charge of meticulously watching each scene being shot and making sure that the written script has not strayed from the original lines. If an actor misses or forgets a word, phrase or emphasis on a line, the script supervisor talks to the director or the director knows right away and the whole scene has to be shot again. Additionally, the script supervisor will document and tag each scene so that it is marked with the number of takes done to actually get the scene.

DIT

DIT is in charge of all digitally filmed playback from a particular scene. This is where digital technology advances dramatically over film. With film you shoot the scene and have to get the film developed to see the scene, lighting and focus. With DIT you can instantly view the scene shot and determine if the scene has all the elements wanted by the director including sound, focus, lighting, script or if there's anything in frame that shouldn't be.

Sound

Sound is in charge of all recorded sound on a given movie set. The sound mixer is the person in charge and has a boom operator working alongside him or her. The boom op is in charge of being right in the middle of a set to record the sound for each particular scene. The boom op carries a large pole boom that reaches approximately sixteen feet out from his hands over the actors to record the dialogue. The mixer is in charge of not only mixing the sound for the dialogue to make sure it cuts well with the final edit but also putting a mike on each talent that is talking on camera for each scene. Sometimes this is a delicate job, to say the least.

Hair & Makeup

Hair and makeup on a movie set play an important role in taking an actor's appearance and shaping it into what might be called for in the script. Whether a war epic or sci-fi film, hair & makeup are magicians of their craft. An actor can be in hair & makeup for hours in order for them to appear on film as if he or she is forty years older. Think about the kind of artistry it takes to make someone look like that and not notice the adjustments on camera.

Wardrobe
Wardrobe department on a set is in charge of stylistically taking the actor into a period in time or particular look for a script through clothing.

Still Photographer
The still photographer is in charge of taking all behind the scenes photos for a movie and/or television show. The studio will then pick any particular shot they want to use as a promotional shot for the movie or show. The still photographer gets paid per shot used. On movie sets is where you will normally see the still photographer. They position themselves right next to the camera, right in the heart of the action to capture a moment. All still photographs you have possibly seen from movie sets in the golden age of Hollywood and modern films have been captured by the still photographer. There is usually a strict nondisclosure on most sets that the crew is not allowed to take pictures. The purpose of that is so that no information nor scene is leaked to the press or social media before the film is released. Only the still photographer is allowed to photograph the film scenes for the studios.

Craft Service
Craft service is a wonderful extra provided by the studios to the working crews throughout any given filming day. There is craft service provided on every set whether it's a

movie, television show, or TV commercial. Craft service provides food all day long to the crew for quick on the go snacks and drinks. Whatever snack you can imagine, is offered free all day long. When you work the kind of hours that movie crews do, hunger and thirst come on very quickly. Studios and productions provide this as a courtesy so that people stay happy and fed at work. And boy, do we! Seriously, it is really awesome, and I never take it for granted.

Catering Truck

One of the best movie perks is the catering truck. Every big movie set has one. And this is different from craft service. Yes, I know. At this point, you are saying to yourself, "Wait a minute, they get snacks all day long and a catering truck?" The answer is yes. Here is how it works. When you show up for a day of work on a set, get there early. Why, you ask? Because the studio funding the movie provides a catering truck with meals for the crew daily for breakfast, lunch, and dinner. And depending on the catering truck, it can be better than a five-star restaurant you would go to for a meal and pay a ton for. You simply show up early and go to the truck where they are serving the food. They will have stations of food that you can choose your meal from, all cooked fresh and on the spot for you. Basically whatever you can think of as your favorite meal, it will be available to you. No joke. Again, I have to say it simply is one of the most amazing perks that come with the job. One word sums it up: awesome!

Note: to give you an idea about how catering trucks came about, studios realized that if the crew took off to go eat meals out and then came back, then two to three hours would be added to each already long day. So production made it so that crews break for meals, on location, with a catered meal. The break is called the Hollywood half, which is a forty-five-minute meal and then you're back to work. On the time card, it is a half hour off the clock.

Locations

The location's department fills a very important position for the studio, screenwriter, and producers. They are the people that deal with all the logistics of a film crew coming into a particular location to shoot. What do I mean by that? You can't just show up to film anywhere you want with three blocks of trucks and hundreds of people. Film permits have to be acquired in each city in order to shoot. Locations crew have a wide range of locations inside and outside of any given city of houses and locations that fill a particular need for a script or look that is needed for a script. They work well in advance—often months—of the crew coming in to shoot to lock down what is necessary for a small or big crew to come into a location or locations to shoot. This includes a wide range of things that most never think about, including parking, permits, how much it will cost to film there, working with the owners of the properties, neighbors, police protection for the crews, how the trucks will get into the locations and where they will park to work, where crews can work on a property and where they are not allowed and dealing with city officials. Most location crew people are not union, but some are part of the teamsters union.

Production

Production is the glue that holds an entire movie together. It is a very important department for the proper running of any given set. There are two main production teams: the office production staff and the set production crew. Both production teams take care of all the fine details for each day of filming and how it will be accomplished. For example, if it is a two hundred million dollar action movie, the studio has a massive amount invested in the movie. Both office and set production have a huge amount of pressure per day to make sure they are moving things along to keep pace with the script, shooting schedule and budget.

Many things can send a picture sideways with regards to budget and schedule. Weather is one. Location is another. Complications with a complicated script is yet another. There are many examples through film history of movies going sideways during filming. One particular one is Apocalypse Now. It is an interesting story and worth Googling.

Set production crew work underneath the director and keep a set running efficiently. The main go to person and ringleader of a film set is the first assistant director. This person plays a pivotal role in making the day's shooting schedule, hours and running each scene for filming. They'll be the person that orchestrates all moving parts on the set of each crew and each scene. On a movie or television set, it is a very complicated position and one that deserves tremendous respect. Under the first AD are a host of positions that support the running of the production. One such person is the key second AD, additional seconds, key set production assistant, and set production assistants. When starting out in the movie business, many people get their first break into the business by starting out as a production assistant. It is generally regarded as the position that most start when they have no experience.

If you get the break into the business this way, remember these key things. Give 150% to every task you are given. Have a great attitude about every task given. Be gritty and outwork your competition. Don't worry about the pay; the money will come. Don't give up and always strive to learn daily. Always pay attention to what is happening on any given set. Look around and figure out what direction in the business that you might want to explore getting into. Once you figure that out, go talk to the key person in that department and express your interest in getting into that department. Ask questions, learn the answers, and then go for it. Hustle and being aggressive are the main aspects to making it in the business. Use the tips above and go at it!

Set Medic

A set medic is a vital part to have on any given set. They are usually EMTs or firefighters moonlighting to make part-time money on the side on a movie set. I can't say enough how important it is to have them on set at all times. With the long hours that movie crews work, people get tired, sick, sometimes hurt and need attention by a trained medic quickly. Thankfully, productions provide for having a medic on films as a precaution.

Precision Drivers

Precision drivers are individuals that are brought in on films to perform high-speed car, motorcycle, or truck scenes. Most of these people are also stunt people but also do this. A lot of precision drivers are used in highly choreographed chase scenes in films. Other things they are brought in for is on television commercials to drive the cars being filmed for an advertisement. Why are they called precision drivers? The name really says it all. Most drivers have extensive experience at high speeds on racetracks, so they know how to handle cars of any caliber. And they know how to precisely move a car, while being filmed, with high-speed cars or cranes in front of them. It can be very dangerous at high speeds with certain filming and exactly why they are brought in to drive the car of choice for the job.

Camera Cranes, Arm Cars, Helicopters, and Drones

Camera cranes are large steel cranes that are usually owned and operated by individual owners. They are brought in on all filming mediums to capture high moving shots that can't be accomplished any other way. There are many types of cranes used in the movie business. Some can reach heights of seventy-five feet and zoom in and out while moving. This kind of filming can produce beautiful wide shots. Usually it will have a crew with a grip or operator on the bucket, an operator on the zoom of the arm, and an operator on the movement of the camera.

Arm cars are also owned and operated by private companies. These particular cars are very unique to the business. They are usually high-speed Porsches, Mercedes, Audis, or even trucks that have a large arm attached to the roof. The arm is weighted in the back and is about twenty feet long with a camera on the end of it. Arm cars are brought in on a film or commercial to follow film high-speed shots that cannot be captured any other way. The arm car follows right next to the action often at speeds approaching one hundred miles per hour while the arm moves up, sideways and around whatever moving action it is filming. Arm cars have a set crew they come to set with: a precision driver, an arm technician, and a camera technician. All three work in unison while the car is in action. It is a very unique piece of movie equipment and one that requires exact precision while filming.

Drones are propelled and electronically controlled devices that can carry a camera up into the air to film a scene. This type of filming is relatively new in the industry over the last few years. The images that a drone can capture are absolutely spectacular. Prior to drones, most of the midair footage was captured by helicopters or planes. Helicopters are widely used in the movie business to get into places that no person or equipment can get to. Helicopter cameras are placed in a rigged bubble casing at the nose of the helicopter or on a line below the helicopter on a rig. In both instances, cameras would film nearly impossible places to capture footage if it were not for this type of machinery. To use helicopters for filming is highly expensive and dangerous but the end footage is spectacular. Drones have made what was once only able to be done via helicopter to be done cheaper, faster, and with equal and often better results. The technology of drones has advanced dramatically over the last few years. Drones are now bigger and can carry larger cameras with amazing stabilization and accuracy. The ability to put a camera on a drone and control it off a fifty-story building to capture a shot in minutes has many benefits for the film industry. Much like helicopter work though, drones are extremely dangerous. When filming around them, take extreme caution and let the techs do their work.

High-Speed Camera Cars

High-speed camera cars are specially designed cars that are used in the movie business to capture particularly dangerous shots on film. These cars are different from arm cars. Arm cars are used for similar purposes. However, high-speed camera cars are exactly that—high speed. These cars are also owned by private companies.

There are only a handful of companies in the world that own these types of cars. Los Angeles is where they are primarily based. The cars are usually highly modified cars both in the engine and body. The cars will be caged out on the exterior usually and stripped of most exterior metal. Which means that they have steel caging around the exterior of the car, kind of like a roll bar on the inside of race cars. The caging is used so that the camera departments, grips, and visual effects can rig cameras to the car on many different parts of the car in order to capture fast action while driving at high speeds. Particular films you will see these cars used on are large action films, such as *Ford v Ferrari*.

Car Prep

Car prep is a department brought in on films to make a car look a specific way. For car commercials, car prep is specifically used to make sure the new cars being filmed to sell to the public look clean at all times. Oftentimes filming will take place through mud, water, dust, and snow. Car prep will be responsible for making sure the car gets clean after each take. The key car prep technician is also responsible for working with the auto transport drivers and coordinating where and when cars will be used for a particular shoot.

Teamsters

The head of the teamsters crew on a set is the gang boss. Teamsters are responsible for all moving vehicles on a movie set. This includes picture cars, star trailers, trucks, pass vans and/or any other mode of transportation that requires movement of equipment or people on a union movie set. This is a very important department on a set in that the gang boss plays an important role in getting trucks close to the set so that crew gear is easily and rapidly workable. Always establish a good working relationship with the gang boss on a movie.

Police Departments and California Highway Patrol (CHP)

I think it's very important to mention protection provided by police departments and security on our film sets—they are union brothers as well. There are a lot of working parts on any given large film. And police departments play a major role in helping coordinate certain things for moving shots and for film crew protection. Let me explain, when shooting a commercial, TV show or movie downtown in big cities, you don't just show up with blocks of trucks, crew and equipment and expect the world to stop because you're shooting a movie. Police departments are contacted by production well ahead of shooting and paid to come out and shut down city streets from traffic for the entire duration of a crew filming there during a given amount of time. If it is a multi move day of locations, they go with us wherever we go and protect us on the streets. As one might guess, there are a lot of people that try to get in close to see what is happening on a given movie. Spectators want to see a certain actor or watch a dangerous stunt scene. The police not only protect the crew but also the public from getting too close to the action so that the crews can work safely.

One of the other major important things to note is that police departments and California Highway Patrol provide protection when a moving or high-speed scene is taken out onto city streets and highways. Often on a given movie, particularly action films, high speed cars, motorcycles, trucks, etc., will be rigged with cameras for a high-speed chase or crash scenes through city streets and on to highways. Once again, this is a highly coordinated and orchestrated effort that takes place between all working police on set, all crew and all production. Before these big scenes take place, all working crew are called to a main meeting place on set where the first assistant director will systematically go over each part of the action scene in detail to all the working crew.

Most of the crew will get to a safe place to watch the action. Oftentimes a chase scene can go blocks and blocks. At that point, police are set in place, along with production assistants to help coordinate keeping anyone from walking or driving into the scene when a high-speed chase with gunfire is taking place. Camera and grip crews are usually right smack in the middle of the action either pushing camera dolly or protecting the camera operator who has his eye on the lens if any of the action goes awry and starts to come at the camera. If that happens, and it does, the camera grip or stunt safety person will immediately yank the camera operator to safety so that he is not injured during the scene.

Some San Francisco motion picture movie lore that many may not know is that the Hells Angels used to be movie security for every movie that came into town for many years. Let's just leave it at that, there was rarely ever a problem with them around. If you don't know who they are, Google them.

Chapter 16

Freelance Additional Crew And Equipment— Cranes, Lighting, Crew

Any additional crew or equipment that is needed on a given set for a day, week or month of a movie has to be hired through the best boys of each department putting a call into the union. If it's a union picture, the union will send out specific technicians to fill the manpower needs of the departments. If it's a non union shoot, the best boys have to rely on who they know in the business and start making calls to those particular freelance technicians seeing if they are available to work.

Chapter 17

Tools For The Freelance Film Technician

Tools are an essential part of your arsenal as a freelance technician. Do yourself a favor and study those around you using tools and pay attention to the good brands.

Essential tools are the following:

- Tool belt: I recommend looking at solid brands such as Occidental Leather Products. In particular, the tool belts they make. They are tough, solid and will last you for years and are well worth the investment.

- Tool pouches: Look to Filmtools.com or Amazon.com for Reyes Tool Pouches. They are solid and affordable. They have many different options to look at.

- Tape measure: Get a good one or get two. They are indispensable to have at work and at your house.

I think I have at least ten. Know how to pull a tape and take measurements. If you don't know how, teach yourself. Use YouTube for all things you don't know.

- Screwdriver: Get a four-in-one, which is a tool that has interchangeable sides between a Phillips screwdriver and a regular screwdriver.

- Channel locks: Many good brands out there for these. Knipex is an amazing brand with many options.

- C wrench: An essential part of all technicians' kits. There are many selections at some of the big home supply stores such as Home Depot and the like. This tool is used widely in the business. It serves many purposes. Usually an eight-inch C wrench should cover your uses.

- A good pocket knife: You will have to make your own judgment on what you consider a good knife. Some recommended brands: Benchmade, Kershaw, Spyderco. Do your research. A good knife can save your life in certain work situations. Know how to use it and know when to use it safely. Make sure you keep your good knife sharp. You can sharpen the knife yourself—go on YouTube for examples—or send it into the manufacturer, and they can do it for you.

- A good matte knife: Personally, I feel the most versatile tool on my belt is this. It can make fine cuts and cut anything rapidly from rope to small items. I use it above all cutting methods.

- Gloves: An essential for the business. Buy a gloves holder on filmtools.com. Leather gloves are a favorite. As well as a glove maker called Dirty Rigger out of England. No matter what craft you end up doing in the business, it is a labor business and you use your hands to craft the art. What I mean is that you need to protect your hands from not only filthy cable that has been dragged through the city streets but also nails from wood, staples, sharp objects, and many other things in the business in the daily working environment that you would not want to touch with your bare hands.

- Hammer: A personal favorite tool. As a grip in the business, we use hammers all the time. We build and have many applications where an instrument of force is needed to get a particular task done. Hammers are an indispensable tool to have in your tool kit. One of my favorite hammers is from Stiletto.com. My particular favorite is the ten-ounce axe handle titanium stiletto hammer. It's light and powerful. When carrying tools all day long on your hips, reduction in weight is key. The longer you're in the business, the more you will see technicians carrying around interesting tools. Ask questions. Ask why they like using one toolmaker over another. Make your own educated decision. But by all means, learn how to use a hammer.

- Electric screw gun and drill: Makita is a solid brand and one of the best, along with DeWalt.

As a grip, carpenter, special effects, props, or electrician, all departments use both of these tools regularly. So it's important that it be part of your tool package. I highly suggest looking into 18v or above as guns of choice. Again, these can be purchased at any one of the major hardware stores in the United States.

- Shoes: This may seem like a silly thing to think about. However, let me assure you it is not. And here is why: When you hit stride in the business with getting work, you will be working a lot. So what does that mean? You will be working long hours and you need to pay attention to the kind of shoes that will give you support to handle those kinds of hours. One thing in the business is that when you are in go mode, everything is moving quickly. You are part of a crew that is part of the working machine to get the movie made. Shoes play an important role as for the most important tool on your body to get you from point A to point B—your feet. So do yourself a favor and look into good tennis shoes with good support. And also look into good working boots for the same purpose. Let me explain how each should be thought about and used.

- As a technician, you do a lot of traveling to locations and stage work. Location work is exactly what it says—locations with all sorts of different terrains. So you must adapt accordingly. For example, if a particular location you show up to for the day's shoot is in the wilderness, and it snowed the night before, and you show up in shorts, T-shirt, Vans, and no weather gear or change of shoes, you can guess the disaster you are going to face within an hour of being there. You will be freezing, unprepared for the terrain and without layers or other gear to change into because you didn't prepare correctly for the job. It pays to ask questions. And it pays to prepare. Oftentimes I will prepare for a job for well over an hour with gear for the next day of shooting and the variables I may come up against. So in the case listed above, the technician should've asked what kind of conditions are we going to be shooting in. And he or she should've brought weather gear, long pants and a good pair of terrain boots to insulate his feet from the cold and protect his ankles from possible sprain on rocks or loose dirt. A good pair of boots or terrain shoes are essential in the business.

- Now we turn our attention to the bulk of where you will likely spend your time in the business—on the streets. Again, it is essential to have a solid pair of shoes that will comfort your feet for the long days on asphalt or cement floor, which you always see on stages. After long days on cement floors, you'll feel your legs big time, so pay attention to my words about good shoes. Change your shoes either once during the day or at least every other day. Have a few pairs of tennis shoes that you change out regularly through your week. Your feet and body will thank you as you start to put the hours in.

- Pants: As a technician on a movie set, you are very lucky in that you can wear pretty much whatever you want. T-shirts, shorts, green hair, funky hats, whatever suits your style. As mentioned before, the work is not about what you wear but how you can creatively perform with your hands and mind. But it's important to note that there are situations where you need to have solid gear and pants fall into this category. There will be certain jobs you do in the business that you will need to have your hands, arms, legs, and feet protected from the elements. That is why it is important to have tough pants to protect your legs. I have found through the years that rip-stop cargo pants seem to fill the category perfectly for me. They are tough, give you options to put plenty of things in your pocket, and last forever. A suggestion on tough pants that are some of the best money can buy is the brand Carhartt. In my opinion, there is no other brand that matches the value you get for the money. And no other brand that is made to withstand work conditions like them.

- Weather gear: This is another massively important category to pay attention to. One thing you will quickly learn working on movies is that weather will rarely stop the work from happening. And some scripts call for weather. So know this going in: You'll work in every type of weather condition possible from desert heat to driving rain, snow, ice, jungles and open ocean conditions. Your job is to already have the gear that will protect you from the elements. My job is to help you figure out what you need starting out and you can build on that as you get more entrenched in the business. The essential must have items are below:

- Rain jacket: There are many great brands out there, so put some research in. REI is a great place to look. If budget is a concern, you can go to search outlet stores in your area that will offer great selection and pricing. Some solid brands that have outlet stores and gear will last you for years are Patagonia and North Face.

- Rain pants: When working in the elements, rain pants are essential. Protection is the name of the game here. Rain pants will serve two purposes. They will keep your pants and legs dry from rain and also insulate you from the cold in snow conditions or mountain cold and brush. Rain pants can get expensive quickly. So one trick I found was going to an army/navy surplus store. Military gear at these stores translates seamlessly into movie business. It's built tough and very inexpensive. Rain pants I got at a surplus store in the Bay Area for $40, and they are US military–issued gore-tex camo pants that are perfect. Similar types of pants at REI or other outdoor stores will run you well over $100. I think you get the idea here.

- Layers: An important aspect of weather conditions are layers. I grew up in scouting and was continually hiking in the Sierras of California with my troop.

One of the biggest things I learned was the ability to have layers of clothes as backup for warmth. One trick to always think about is that if you have layers, you can always peel them off if you get too hot. If you don't have layers, you will suffer from lack of warmth and learn your lesson very quickly. So what are the most effective layers? The most effective layering goes underneath your rain jacket. The rain jacket protects you from the rain and wind. Under the rain jacket you have numerous layer options. A great standby is a fleece zip-up or pullover jacket. These jackets will keep your chest warm from the cold. Under the fleece you should have additional lighter layers of either another pull quarter zip type of warmth layer. Under that you should have a T-shirt and a long-sleeve thermal under that. You should also have thermals for your legs in cold conditions.

- Sunglasses: When working outside, crews are in the sun a lot, so it's important to have good UV-cutting sunglasses to protect your eyes. Trust me when I say that spending a bit extra on a good pair of sunglasses will pay dividends always.

- Hats: Again, it may seem obvious but hats serve a major purpose when working in the elements. So having a wide assortment of hats for different types of environments you will be working in is important. Everyday baseball caps and wide brimmed hats serve to block the sun and cowboy hats are also a great option.

- A portable tool case or Pelican case: Over time you will start to accumulate a wide assortment of tools above and beyond your tool belt. With that comes the question as to how you bring these tools to a given job without breaking your back and also in a compact case. There are many options out there offered by companies that make tool bags with wheels. A particular case that has become very popular with technicians is the Pelican 1510 case. It has wheels, a pull up handle, can be brought on a plane and stored above, comes with many options to layout the inside, can be locked, is tough as nails and to me a fantastic option for carrying and protecting all your gear.
- Author tip: I recommend spending a little extra to buy better tools than not. If you choose the latter, the tools will either fail on you when you most need them or break, causing you to spend twice as much to buy something else when you could've just bought good tools to begin with. Food for thought.

Chapter 18

Go At It And Have Fun!

Once you have finished reading this book, now it's time to put a plan into action. Use this book as a reference. Constantly come back to it for the how-to's on how to go about your journey. Keep it with you and reread each section that applies to where you are in the journey. Be aggressive and go at it! And get ready for a wild ride!

Chapter 19

Other Useful Information And Nuggets Of Wisdom

- Get your foot in the door any way you can.

- Outsmart your competition—pretty much says it all. It's who you know as much as what you know.

- Go learn. No matter what age.

- Meet the Gaffer–search out on YouTube. This is a superb free source for motion picture technician information.

- Remember to always have balance in your work and personal life. Never miss the important moments in life that you will never get back, such as watching your kids grow up, weddings, once in a lifetime trips with friends, and being there for the people who care and love you. Work will always be there. People and moments will not.

- It's only a movie; you're not saving lives. Remember to have fun doing what you do! And remember how lucky you are to be able to do it!

- Be calm in the eye of the storm.

- Once you start getting steady work, you have mentors all around you. Watch the smart, savvy veterans and learn. Ask a lot of questions to get the answers. This is absolutely essential to all entering the business and all that are already entrenched. There is much to learn each and every day on any given set, whether you are new or a seasoned vet.

- Have tough skin. What do I mean by that? The ability to work through tough situations. Whatever the situation is—weather or working with difficult people. One of the greatest aspects of the business, whether dealing with one or all of the above elements is that the job will end at some point, whether that is three days or three months. So you know you are not stuck in a challenging situation for a great length of time. Your ability to have tough skin will serve you well in the business. Work hard, have a good attitude and use many of the other tips within this book daily and you will have an amazing journey.

Acknowledgments

I want to thank the numerous people who reached out and gave me support and also the many who just simply offered to help in any way they could. Thank you, one and all. Additionally, I am forever grateful for the love and support of my family and friends in my life who have been with me along my journey.

About The Author

Joe is also a father, entrepreneur, Eagle Scout and UCLA graduate with other passions including adventure travel, music, art and enjoying his children.

www.ingramcontent.com/pod-product-compliance
Lightning Source LLC
Chambersburg PA
CBHW061802070526
44586CB00023B/2676